THE
LASCAUX REVIEW
VOLUME 7
ANNO DOMINI 2020

THE
LASCAUX REVIEW
VOLUME 7
ANNO DOMINI 2020

edited by
Stephen Parrish
Wendy Russ

The Lascaux Review

Editor
Stephen Parrish

Managing Editor
Wendy Russ

Senior Editors
Marissa Glover
Camille Griep

Editors
Angela Kubinec
Isabella David McCaffrey
Laurel Miram
Shannon Morley-Ragland
Erica Orloff
Lisa Pellegrini
Sarah Specht

ISBN: 978-1-7344966-2-8

Cover design by Wendy Russ. Cover art by William Adolphe Bouguereau: "Berceuse (Le coucher)," oil on canvas, 1873.

Lascaux Books
www.lascauxbooks.com

Contents

continued next page

Short Fiction

Creative Nonfiction

Gaze

by Alexandra Grimm

The first time it happens, you are eleven and walking alongside your mother. The summer air is humid—like down against your faces—so when the men in the passing pickup truck scream out all they want to do with your bodies, their voices arrive slow and elongated through the thick heat.

You look up at your mother. *Maybe they meant that for you*, you say. You have always thought your mother beautiful enough to elicit the cries of strangers.

Not for me, baby, she says, and her fine face darkens as she studies you.

*

Impossible to count the second, third, fiftieth times, the howls of men spanning all four seasons, and every kind of outfit you could throw together. Sometimes they call from close enough to touch you. Sometimes they touch you.

In your twenties, a man follows you for nine city blocks. He abandons the chase when he realizes your destination: the public library. Men may have ideas on what you should do with your serious mouth, your stretchy, long legs, but don't get it twisted—no one actually wants to fuck a bookworm.

*

And then a cold night in bed with Matthew, whom you will later marry.

In a playful wrestling match, he goes for your armpits, which he knows can be tickled to the point of pain. You are laughing through your nose when he says what you have heard so many times before: *You know you want it.*

You cry angry tears, shout, *Never say that to me again!* Though you know for certain he will heed your demand, when he holds you afterward you feel brittle, like the helicopter leaves you collected as a girl, which crumbled easily and had stems that would not snap.

Joshua

by Jordana Jacobs

Inside the ovaries of my husband's grandmother, Sylvie, resided an egg the size of a grain of sand that would have been Hannah, my brilliant and accomplished mother-in-law, proficient in five languages and fluent in three. And, as girl babies are born with all the eggs they will ever have, granular Hannah was carrying all the eggs she would never be born with inside her infinitesimal ovaries. One of those specks was my Joshua.

Sylvie was killed the same week that Anne Frank perished from Typhus, which was also the week before liberation at Bergen-Belsen. And so, with Sylvie, perished the ovary, and all the eggs inside it, and all the grandchildren that would follow.

That's how Joshua and I came to never meet in 1984 at my Socialist-Zionist summer camp. If we had, we would have avoided each other for the first three weeks of camp anyway, a subconscious protection from an adult future for which we were not ready. Inside my 12-year-old body, a body I never thought about unless a scab itched my leg or a smart aleck put ice down the back of my shirt, nested an ovary, and inside that ovary lay all the eggs I would ever have. Two of those eggs—eggs that would inconveniently give me cramps and drop into my underwear one morning in my mid-thirties—were our twins, Ruby and Gabriel. Joshua and I were not ready for all of that and so we barely looked each other in the eye.

On the last Shabbat of the summer, the night deferred hookups came due, Joshua would ask me to take a walk with him by the lake. There, we'd kiss for the first time, tentatively letting our tongues touch, and his breath would be hotter than I was expecting and I'd picture the steam that rose from manholes and how, as a child, my mother believed they were heating the city, and then, as he pushed his mouth a little harder against mine, I'd wonder if that pushiness distinguished a girl kiss from a boy kiss.

We'd lose touch. Or we'd date another three consecutive years. We'd marry young, on a kibbutz, poster children for the Movement. Scratch that. We'd meet again in our late twenties when he was catering a public relations luncheon I was attending for Pfizer. Or he'd see my online dating profile and suggest we catch up. At first, I wouldn't be able to get past his Long Island accent and, though he couldn't verbalize it until much later, he'd be put off by my resistance to adventure and my fear of anything that dramatically altered my body temperature. At first, I'd be dazzled by how wise he'd

4

grown, how intentional he was about building a relationship together. At first, I thought I could push him away with words hurtful and spectacularly true. At first, I was hesitant to date a Jewish man, insisting that it was my biological imperative to mate outside the stagnant waters of the Ashkenazi gene pool. At first, I couldn't believe how lucky I was to have found him. At first, it was casual. At first, I was painfully jealous of his previous girlfriend, convinced that he worshiped her body in a way he never would mine. At first, we'd debate whether to abort the long-awaited fetus diagnosed with Gaucher disease. At first, we'd travel together to Honduras and we'd break up the moment we returned. At first, people would think we were brother and sister and we'd shock them with almost pornographic PDA.

That's how Sylvie's chromosomes would fail to entwine with mine. There was an empty bunk bed in the boy's cabin, mainly used for drying towels when it was raining outside. I'd sit in their cabin watching them play Crazy Eights, half waiting to be kicked out, and I would be very, very still, listening for my Joshua.

If It Were You
by Kyra Kondis

L et's just say that you volunteered your boyfriend, Dave, to be turned into a chameleon by an illusionist at a bar in Atlantic City. Let's say the illusionist's name was Dexter the Dangerous, and he had on this sparkly purple tuxedo, and you'd never seen an illusionist before, so obviously you wanted to do it. And let's say that Dave was being stubborn about this—really, let's just say that Dave was always kind of stubborn—the kind of person who would come over and refuse to take off his shoes at the door because he didn't think they were dirty, or drop his phone out of the car window to prove it wouldn't break. Let's say that this kind of attitude just made you want to see the illusionist even more.

And let's just say that Dave only came into the bar with you in the first place because you were like, "I see someone I know in there!" and ran inside, and he was all, "Jesus, Sarah, chill." And let's say you were getting tired of his condescending tone. And Dexter—let's say that Dexter the Dangerous was in this bar doing a card trick for some girls from Rutgers, and Dave was saying, "Where's the person you know?" and you were saying, "Shut up, Dave," because then Dexter was pulling a card out of his mouth and asking, "Is that your card?" and the Rutgers girls were squealing and jumping up and down and clapping their hands. So maybe you decided to go up to Dexter the Dangerous after that, and he was smiling at you in his shining purple suit and saying he had the *best* trick for you, and you couldn't see Dave behind you but you were sure he was rolling his eyes, so you said to Dexter, "Dave will do it!"

And now, well, let's just say that you aren't really sure what to do with Dave now. Because maybe you panicked and left with him clinging to your arm, and you bought him a tank and some green plants and a UV light and a spray bottle of distilled water, and you can't find a way to contact Dexter the Dangerous anywhere on the Internet. And maybe you feel a little bit weird keeping him as a pet, but you'd also feel weird selling him to someone else, and you know that if you released him into the wild, he'd have, well, no chance. And let's say that even though you can flush your toilet whenever you want to now, you miss person-Dave a little bit—maybe you miss how he used to make really good fettucine alfredo, or let you wear his favorite baseball hat with a ship in a bottle embroidered on the front, or sometimes even bring you little gifts from the Trader Joe's he managed. Maybe now you're realizing that you might never find anyone like person-Dave again.

Let's just say it was you. Would you set him loose some-where, somewhere that seemed safe, and watch his small, green body skitter away until it was just a speck? Would you keep him in your living room and feed him mealworms and wonder if saying his name to him would help him remember himself? Would you try to sell him to PetSmart and hope that he doesn't end up in a kindergarten class somewhere, be-cause he never really liked kids much, and kindergarteners don't know how to care for a chameleon, especially not one like Dave?

What would you do?

"If It Were You" originally appeared in *Matchbook*.

Three Pictures of My Father That Survived the Great Divorce Purge of 1977

by Kathryn Kulpa

1. Church Stairs

It's someone's wedding. Not his own. He looks too happy, caught midstep on the stairs, his loosey-goosey legs, foot tilted, lifting his hand to shade his eyes. He moved with a kind of feline grace, not so much tiger as alley cat, forever on the prowl. Even his eyes were like a cat's, green in some lights, brown in others, almost yellow if you caught him in headlights, in flashlight, in a camera's flash in the hands of a private detective as he left a motel room with some other man's wife.

Women called him handsome mostly because of those eyes. I remember it, that look they loved. Eyelids heavy, half closed, like he'd just turned over in bed and she was the first thing he saw. He's flashing a grin, dark suit, skinny tie, all Rat Pack sharp. *You sly dog! You devil you!* Your dad's a *hot sketch*, some old lady at a wedding told me once. Old, young. Little girls in ankle socks. He'd teach them card tricks. Their mothers would drift over and freshen his drink.

I was a mistake, Aunt Eileen blurted out once after a wake, when she was well into the Jameson's. My mother was supposed to go to school. Did I know how talented she was? Had I ever seen her drawings?

She helps me with art projects for school, I said.

Geez, the waste of it, Eileen said.

2. Training Wheels

I'm straddling my first two-wheel bike, standing tippy-toe, my mouth in a wide grin showing the tooth I'd lost. My father is holding up the training wheels, giving a thumbs-up. He must have just taken them off. I'm told my mother argued against this. I should remember it, but I don't: there were so many arguments. I'm holding the handlebars with one hand, giving the same thumbs-up with the other.

My father is wearing a jeans jacket and some kind of newsboy cap; this must have been when his hair first started to thin. There's something apologetic about him, something sidewise in his smile. My mother must have taken the picture. I don't have the scar I would have later, the half-inch slash like a cleft chin. I don't have a broken collarbone. Not yet. I have a bike with a pink banana seat. The streamers on the handlebars are pink and white and silver and there's a white plastic basket in the front with plastic daisies in it, only the stems of those daisies were some kind of paper wrapped around sharp wire.

I remember the trip to the emergency room, how they took me in a room and wouldn't let my parents in, my mother's voice frantic, arguing with the nurse. The nurses asking me what happened. *I couldn't stop. I hit this car. I fell off my bike.* Asking me again. *Do your parents ever hurt you?*

3. Office Party Polaroid

There's a game I play with this one. Pick the mistress out of the Christmas party picture.

It's my father the way I never saw him. My father at work. He's traded in his suit for a bulky, Aztec-patterned sweater, more Starsky than Hutch. Crepe-paper streamers hang from drop ceilings, tiny artificial trees on desks, a red-nosed Santa taped to the wall. All the men in their bellbottom pants and wide ties, all the women in their tan pantyhose and red or green polyester blouses tied at the neck with bows.

A pussy bow, someone told me that style is called.

Which one is she? I never found out but I'd stare at the picture, trying to match a face to that voice I'd hear on the phone: *Is your father home? Something's come up at work. Oh, no, just tell him to check in with the office when he gets a chance.* At the oddest hours, Saturdays, past nine on weeknights when no one could still be working.

I eliminated the woman with oversize glasses and a frosted wig and the grandmother-looking lady with the reindeer sweater. Was it the feathered-haired one with boots who was sticking out her tongue for the camera? The skinny one with the Carol Brady shag: wasn't there something fake and taunting about her smile? Was it door number one or door number two? If I had to testify, which would I choose?

The affair was over by the time the divorce was final. The women I'd sometimes see at awkward weekend dinners were younger, more transitory; their faces blurred in my memory, less substantial than a washed-out Polaroid. The heart attack came in bed, but there was no buxom secretary to complete the picture. My father died alone.

Limerence

by A.D. Lauren-Abunassar

I bought a radio (blue) at the yard sale down the street. No one walked with me. I walked by myself. The trees were not pleasant company on account of the rain and all their drip-drip-dripping on my favorite (blue) hat. Still, I talked to them as I walked down the sidewalk. *Isn't it ironic,* I said, all Alanis Morissette as I hopped over a sidewalk crack, long and veiny with a little cluster of (blue) weeds cropping up through the mortar.

Isn't it ironic, a yard sale in the rain?

But when I got to the yard sale down the street, I found the whole thing had been moved inside the (blue) house so it wasn't really a yard sale at all. More of a here's-my-living-room-with-plastic-covered-sofas-and-a-smelly-fireplace-sale. I was so cold and shivering by the time I stumbled through the door, pat-pat-patting my rain boots on the front (blue) mat, that my hands felt like seltzer water. All tingly and vocal and asking for gloves. *I've left them at home, I'm sorry,* I told my hands. *Who thought spring rain could be so cold?*

It didn't take me long to find the radio, hiding behind a blender whose *Pulse, High, Low,* button labels had all rubbed clear off. I patted the blender on the head but it was the radio I really wanted. I got it for a dollar fifty, which was the price I wanted to pay, but I was disappointed because the owner wouldn't haggle to get there and I so wanted to haggle. She just threw up her hands and said *whatever you want to pay. I'm done with her.* She didn't want to talk about money, or the strange weather we're having, or the new neighbors who've moved in across the way.

I carried my radio home and put it on my bedside table right next to your picture. I got to feeling really sad, wishing I could hear you singing that song about the (blue) moon. *It's just a (blue) moon kind of day isn't it?* I told my pillow though she was sound asleep. I turned to my radio and fiddled with the knobs but no sound came. I thought maybe a dollar fifty had been a terrible mistake and I hit the cd-deck on the top of the radio over and over like I was burping a baby.

You don't have to hit so hard, said a voice.

Who was that? I asked no one in particular. My coffee mug was drinking coffee. My desk chair was (blue) bird watching, my books were all experimenting with transcendental meditation, as books will do. I knew none of them were the source of the voice.

Who else? said the voice. *Your radio.*

I won't spend time trying to convince you I was entirely surprised. I wasn't surprised. I was excited. I introduced myself to my radio, my radio to me and I asked her to play the song you used to sing me when I'd eaten too much Chinese food and my stomach felt swollen and hard as a tombstone. She complied. No complaints. I sang along to the song and she sang along to the song and when it was over, we both told each other how much we enjoyed each other's voices.

Do you ever get lonely? I asked the radio.

I'm a radio, the radio replied. *Of course I get lonely.*

I wanted to ask her what loneliness felt like when you're a radio. Was it kind of like sitting in a room made of paper? Was it kind of like being filled with a hundred (blue) lights all firing off at once? Was it kind of like waking up to find all your old love letters photocopied and thumbtacked to each wet-tree on your street, a big red ex scratched through each *all my love* or *soon I'll be home.*

But instead, I turned her to look at your picture and I didn't say anything at all.

Anyway. Since you've gone away, I've been keeping downright busy. Going to not-quite-yard sales. Making friends with my radio and asking her to play me the song you used to sing when you sang to my belly. And by the time you get back, I'll have memorized all the words. And I can tell you all about the strange weather we've been having and the (blue) (blue) light that hits your side of the bed in the morning.

Wapiti Nocturne
by Douglas W. Milliken

For a month or more after our mum percolated a long dramatic breath, sighed it off like a steaming radiator and never took another, my sister and I did something like live in the forever-year-old farmhouse where we had allegedly grown up. Who can say what we thought we were doing there. We certainly weren't cleaning up the collected mass of a lifetime our mum in her perdurable inquisition had assembled, records labeled in foreign languages and countless volumes on the histories of countries we'd never heard of before or since, folio upon folio of sepia and silver-print photographs showing people who apparently were our progenitors engaged in the rites of self-preservation, a kitchen and pantry chock-a-block with brined mandrake and currant jams and bufo butters dating back to before either one of us was born. Certainly we weren't corroborating among this orphaned paraphernalia on our obvious common loss. If we were nuns, we'd be the kind committed to a permeating order of silence. But I suspect, then and now, ours was the only sisterhood who'd ever admit us in.

Mum died in the last days of October, leaving—among other things—a lot of fall-time chores incomplete. We filled our days splitting and stacking the remaining cords of maple and birch rounds, banking the foundation with vinyl sheeting and junky bales of hay, digging and stowing beets and gentian in the musty crypt of the cellar. No talking. Nights silent by the woodstove while nightwind rattled the nude trees outside, making haunting nightmusic to which we couldn't sing along. I wasn't yet aware that my gap year before college was to be a lifetime appointment. It'd be a few months still before my sister took to grumbling about the dubious promises of a baby-faced Army recruiter. We were holding still, I'm sure, for fear of what might happen if we dared break what was still.

But what is stillness but a denial of all that's real? Even the steam and shrivel of the dead can't be slowed to a stop. What ended our attempted stasis of not talking and not really grieving was an owl and a mouse and an elk's marble eyes. So how's that for some natural witchery? An early December night like any other but not really night yet—I guess whatever winter preparations that day had us aching and tired early, because there was still some Disney-magic light left outside like a thick beeswax candle hiding the flame its wick-belly contained—and at our rocking-chair nightstations by the woodstove and window we saw first the outlines of basswood and aspen black against the wax-dusk sky, then the demigod mystery of a barred owl descending with a mouse pinched through in its beak, in a talon-flurry trying and failing to perch on the closed window's sill, then in the instant the bird gave up—vaporizing back into the deepening twilight—the elk's primordial head appeared. And by this I don't mean to say that the beast emerged somewhere within the wide lens of the window's scope: no, the elk's head, from rack to bell, filled the entirety of the window. As if the bull had sidelong approached the house expressly to peek inside. Which is exactly what he did. Examining us each with one appraising black eye like a shooter no boy wants to lose—taking our measure with the idiot judgment only an animal can levy—then lifting his head and walking on by, the geography of his red hide for a moment defining all the outside world we could see. Because the window was a door the beast saw fit to open, then to shut. When he passed, the candlelight of the sky was gone, the coming threat of dark replaced by true first dark, first stars, first grief.

Then again, ripe as we were for a change, anything, I'm sure, could have stepped forth from the dusky unknown and shocked us into seeing signs. Yet I wonder, does it ever get tiring, being mistaken as a symbol of profound and consistent might? Even now, I can still clearly see it, how the pierced mouse writhed in the owl's piercing beak, no urgency left in its struggle, its mournful mouth open to cry a cry I'll never hear.

Our sisterly cloister disbanded soon after. My sister one morning hung up her ax, moved back into her apartment above the gas station on the borderland highway, and that was that. I managed a way of staying alive among the cryptic wreckage of our mum's life. Eventually, we all went away. But here's the thing about memory: try to hold on or try to let go, you carry it with you throughout. You leave home and travel to unimagined cities and bedrooms, discover yourself enacting sins and virtues impossible to anticipate, and through it all like a penny in your pocket rides a valedictory light and a preying owl looking for one second's rest and an elk whose curiosity is too ancient and bold for our mortal hearts to ever comprehend. The death scream of a mouse muted behind glass. Don't think for a second it's in the past. We leave nothing behind. We just forget the burden is not light.

When We Believed
the World Wouldn't End

by Benjamin Cutler

After the final harvest, the forecast
called for freezing temperatures
and the end of this winsome world.

We have never trusted doomsday
news, but this new winter had been born
a living, wet, and hungry thing. We could feel

its ice-watered tongues pushing through
the walls, searching for our mouths. *Stand
here*, I said, *stand here and look.* The silvered

sun still knew itself and breathed its yellow
name through the window glass. *Wait. Listen,*
I said. *Doesn't it sound like our last warm day*

of picking? Yes: the apple orchard in fall,
the master's cider-drunken sleep, our love-
making behind the hives. You loved

the colony's scent: wax-ripened bread and apple-
blossom gold. The bees' thrum made you horny,
you said, because it was a music more ancient

than love. Our bodies became themselves then—
all petal-bloom and honey-gleam—each spill
and blood-warm bud a blessing of skin and sun

on our tongues. The memory sung, we stepped
from the window's dying glow into the stone-
blue shadow—the dark of a winter-dead hive,

the dark of an ice-shattered tree. The tired sun
grew hoarse and the frosted tongues licked
their teeth. When I reached for your hand, I found

a blackened apple frozen to its branch. *The forecast
was right after all*, I tried to say, but my tongue
was brittle with cold, the words ice in my throat.

Survival Guide for a Depressive

by Lisa Dordal

Draw a map, out of scale,
to the house where you grew up.
Draw snow, then rain.
Draw your mother
riding a horse in a state
she never mentioned.
Nebraska, perhaps.

Pretend you are the silhouette
of a woman you do not know.
Or a girl who smells faintly of lime.

Learn to hunt beetles and worms.
Declare yourself part shaman,
part musical bow.

Lie down beside the remains
of an old fire and pray
to the god you believe in. Pray
to the one that you don't.

Think of buried things:
teeth tucked into fissures;
craniums and seven small vases;
a sandal engraved with birds
and the words
Wear in good health.

Raise your voice
to the Milky Way—
call it winter road
or backbone of night.

Watch a flock of birds—
so many brains
all at once—in the sky.
Notice how the sky
begins at your feet.

Draw three doors
on a sheet of paper. Look back
before you enter.

"Survival Guide for a Depressive" originally appeared in
DMQ Review.

When You Are Invisible, You Can Say Anything

by Valentina Gnup

At two in the morning through plaster walls,
I hear the neighbors' whispers and groans.
I hear the thunder of helicopters—
giant blackbirds without hearts,
the wild soundtrack of urban living.

Branches outside my window are like the fingers
of old women, stiff knuckles tap on the glass.
I study my own hands, imagine secrets buried in my
limbs—tight buds waiting for April,
the distant memory of leaves.

At sixty-one, I count and recount my remaining summers.
When I face anyone on the street, I notice
how their eyes slip over me without pausing.
When did I become ashamed to exist?

They tell me at this age I can say anything—
so I tell you I'm losing control to the student in the back
row with the low voice who dares me to go further,
to push the invisible ropes we line up against.
I'm supposed to be his teacher—I can't tell him
I've always bounced from one bad answer
to the next wrong move,
that I've followed people across the whole country—
and what man is worth all those Tennessees?

I never had a brother but I wanted one,
wanted to catch glimpses of his hairy belly
when he would casually lift his shirt to scratch or stretch,
wanted to inhale the animal scent of his bedroom
and watch him shoot free throws on the driveway.

I can say I wish my father had treated me
like a man treats a young woman.
He was kind and respectful, never crossed
a line that any good life insurance salesman
wouldn't cross, but I wanted more.

I heard a man read a poem about how he drove by
a burning house, watched the arc of water
from the firefighter's hose and silently celebrated
that his own house wasn't on fire.

I tell myself remember the passions you've known,
the man with the bluest eyes in the world
lifted you onto his lap in one move,
you surrendered, ignored every commandment,
coveted strange gods and ran into the burning house.

The Work in Progress

by Jonathan Greenhause

When compiling
a grocery list, start small: Write
the milk, the OJ,

the mixed greens. Then progressively
add the black-market baby,
the nuclear arms treaty,

the alien gestating
in your chest cavity. At the market,
remember you're only here

to avenge your father
by attacking his average life: He dreamt
he'd eventually pen

the Great American Novel
but wound up practicing law, always
earnestly practicing.

By the registers, strip off your clothes
& metamorphose
into who you dreamed of becoming

before you became what you are:
The end result of a list,
having carefully added

a talented spouse,
a beautiful bouncing
inflatable baby, a delicate package

of lies. Whenever
compiling a list, be sure you're ready
to compromise.

"The Work in Progress" originally appeared in *Jewish Currents*.

Serving
by Kari Gunter-Seymour

Remember that time your dog died and I didn't tell you
for months because you had deployed
and George Bush was shouting, *Bring it on*
and we were all thinking that Korea was fixing to blow.
But when I emailed to say we were headed for West
Virginia, you fired back, *Mom, where is Annie?*
and I had to say she was hit by a car.
I sent brownies loaded with black walnuts
from the old home place.

Or when you called me from Iraq asking me to
talk to people about donating shoes and I told you it was
hopeless because of the Tsunami,
everyone was already donating.

You said *Hell with that* and your unit threw in their
paychecks and bought all those families
just outside Fallujah new shoes off the Internet.
I made two hundred popcorn balls wrapped in wax paper.

Or that February you came home for R&R, so sad and sick.
I baked your favorite, meatloaf, and you said you couldn't
possibly, but I gave you doe-eyes so you ate and threw up
all night, into the next day, saying over and over
Sweet Jesus, please, make it stop
and I knew you weren't talking about the meatloaf.

Or the day after Sergeant Crabtree went to Vegas
and blew his head off in the hotel bathroom,
while here at home your best friend got arrested
for selling narcotics and you said neither one of them
needed to and maybe wouldn't have if you'd been there.
So I shipped molasses cookies thick with Crisco frosting,
all the way to Kandahar.

Or the afternoon your farm boy fingers
tried to clamp the artery on that precious baby girl,
near the valley of Arghandab, while her father
screamed for Allah and blood soaked your uniform
when you hugged her to you as she passed.
I drenched that fruitcake in brandy for three days.

But mostly it was the night your daughter was born
and we locked eyes across the birthing room.

I thought to myself, skillet-fried chicken with candied sweet potatoes, fried okra, lima beans with bacon, cornbread and aunt Margaret's hot fudge cake. We used the good dishes and grandpa Oris said the blessing.

"Serving" originally appeared in *Still: The Journal.*

The Facts

by Patricia Hale

It was the boy who lived down the street,
my own brother's age but not like him—
tougher, quieter, more dangerous,
the kind of boy you knew had a blade
in his back pocket instead of a comb;
whose mother was so thin and faded
you couldn't even make out the print of her dress;
whose father packed his bags and moved
to Wheeling, West Virginia,
where he already had another wife,
another life, another pack of kids;
a boy who quit school and moved out at 17
to an apartment in the city where they said
he kept a gun on the mantle
and a stash in the top dresser drawer;
who a couple years later, when a cop asked

did he ever take a bath, stuck out his chin
and said he never took nothing;
the boy whose arrest photo I cut
from the Sunday Pittsburgh Press
and mounted in my blue leatherette album.
He was the one who saw me there
on the bottom of the pool, stunned
from a wild elbow to the head,
gazing around me calmly surprised
by the thought I might be drowning.
He was the one who grabbed my wrist,
pulled me to safety, then without a word,
went back to his friends on the other side,
leaving me breathless.

"The Facts" originally appeared in the *Connecticut River Review*.

She Knows the Names of Shells
by Karen Paul Holmes

Now that she lives on Sanibel Island,
my sister teaches me the shells.
Along the tideline, she picks up one,
a kitten's paw—
shows me its ribs like toe bones.
Calico scallop, baby's ear, pear whelk.
She bends for broken
bits too, keeps them for their color
and pattern, the pocked and sea-battered
slipped into pant pockets.

What makes us hold on to beauty,
the pink swirls and green veins? Collections
lined on a tray like Eileen's
—one perfect sample of each.
The rest, she glues to painted canvas—

coral, nine-armed starfish, seagrape leaves
brushed with pearlized white, as if still lit
by the lamp of sun.

I try hard not to bring shells home,
no need for even one more
memory in a Haviland bowl.
Eileen and I know how to hold
this time even when we're a state apart.

Heads lowered in "the Sanibel stoop,"
we walk, reminding ourselves
to look up. At cloud swirls, the vein of horizon.
Terns and the rare skimmers lift before us,
follow the south-curving shore.
We turn north,
scan the slanted lines of sea grass
for our path home, where beach becomes
dune becomes land.

"She Knows the Names of Shells" originally appeared in *Valparaiso Poetry Review.*

A Body in Motion
by Edison Jennings

In this compact piedmont coal town, a hospital,
a walk-in wedding chapel, and a funeral home
are all within a half-mile radius of steep-grade roads,
and you can get on a bicycle outside the maternity ward,
push-off vigorously, merge on to Court Street,
lean a hard right to the Happy Bells Wedding Chapel,
wave as you pass my house, then, looking both ways,
dash lickety-split across the street to the Frost Funeral Home,
never pedaling once, while the whole contraption,
of which you are a part, frame and wheels, bone and heart,
all that makes you quick, whirs for once in concert,
so brief and sweet you lift your arms and glide, hands free,
the last few yards and come to rest at the place
that drew you from the start, downhill all the way.

"A Body in Motion" originally appeared in *TriQuarterly*.

On Learning That My Daughter's Rapist Has Been Taught to Write a Poem

by Katharyn Howd Machan

About his sadness.
About how the moon hung full
that morning, every morning

his fist felt like a beast
tethered and tied against its need
to howl and hit and hurt.

About how he needed
the good dope, too, and how she
stared at the gleam in his eyes

with mockery, goddammit, taunts
he wasn't full man enough
to bend the bars of their gray

days, this city of sunless grins.
About how good it felt to take
her pussy, her twat, her tight dark

hole and turn her inside out
like a star (oh, his teacher talked
of similes) and how he hasn't

seen a sky from edge to edge
since somehow he got put in here
where metal clangs and cotton clings

and generous souls who offer classes
have to leave their belts with buckles
behind them at the wordlessly locked door.

Five Short Poems
by Simon Perchik

*

These gravestones left stranded
warped from sunrises and drift
—they need paint, tides, a hull

that goes mouth to mouth
the way seagulls come by
just to nest and preen

though death is not like that
it likes to stand and lean
scattering its brilliant feathers

—look up when you open the can
let it wobble, flow into you
till wave after powerful wave

circles as face to face
and your own loses itself
already beginning to harden.

*

You need more, two sinks
stretching out as constant handfuls
though each arm is lowered

by the darkness you keep at the bottom
—a single cup suddenly harmless
not moving –this rattle you hear

is every child's first toy
already filled with side to side
that's not the sound a small stone makes

trying to let go the other, stake out
a cry all its own, fill it
on your forehead without her.

*

You collect grass the way each star
Eats from your hand, trusts you
To become a nest for the afternoons

Not yet at home in the air, named for nights
That circle down, want to be night again
Take root in your chest as the ripples

From the long stone fallen into the water
Teaching it to darken, to stay
Then smell from dirt then shadows

—side by side you dead pull the ground closer
—with both arms need these whispers warm
already the place to ask about you.

*

And though this stone is small
it has more than the usual interest
in the dead, waits among tall grasses

and water holes, smells the way dirt
still warms the afternoons
that no longer have a place to stay

—you leave a nothing in the open
letting it darken to remember
where you buried the Earth

as if the sun could not be trusted
to take back in its light
and by yourself turn away.

*

You read out loud the way this bed
listens for the makeshift seam
loosening each night down the middle

and though there is no sun
you peel off page after page
as if underneath what you hear

are her eyes closing—word by word
louder and louder—you think it's air
that's falling—everything in your hands

is too heavy, becomes a shadow, covers her
with a single finger pointed at the ceiling light
what's no where on the pillow or closer.

My Broken Brain
by Angie Ellis

I keep a list of songs I know well, so that if I get dementia people can reach the *real me* hidden inside my broken brain. I imagine myself slumped in a chair, wisps of fluffy, non-directional hair on my bony head while some distant grandson fumbles through his futuristic music provider (an implant in his pinky or a button on his tinted Bono-glasses). He finds a song, let's say *Poker Face* by Lady Gaga, and my head jerks up like strings are attached. I smile. I say something retro like, "Dude, I dropped my iPhone in the toilet again." He smiles back and says, "What's a toilet?" (They've fixed the issue of consumption and waste in the future—injections. I don't know this *for a fact*, of course, but there's a good chance it'll happen.)

Ben says stop being weird. I say planning for your future is weird? He inches away from me, tired of my ideas. I can tell he'll leave in the next three months, maybe less. I'll slip the note I've already written into his shirt pocket and pat it three times, like a wise father bestowing a gift of money. The note says *This was fun, don't forget your humongous bag of Peanut Butter M&Ms* (Costco sale). Then I'll kiss him on the cheek and hope he smells my pheromones. Not because I want him to stay, but because, goddamnit, don't be an asshole. I'll say see you around, maybe I'll wink. I'll wear the t-shirt that's so thin my nipples show. (It's hanging in the closet, I've dried myself with it like an animal spreading its scent.)

At work I keep ziplock bags of flour in the back of the cupboard, adding spoonfuls every day (I work at Zeke's Treats—home of the original bacon donut). When they get full I bring the little bags home and put them in a large rubbermaid bin in case there's ever a flour shortage. And there will be. Have you seen the wheat fields of Uttar Pradesh? Withered and dry, so dry you can hear the wind crack the stalks. This sounds like snapping sticks and crushing M&Ms and *raging fire* (this is how I imagine it, understand, there is no way to prove this to you). Once my bin is full I will bake a giant cake and start over, because old flour tastes stale and results in a denser crumb. Then I'll throw a party. The invitations are made and sit in the top drawer of my dresser with my undies. I've addressed them (organized) and stamped them (good financial planning) but inside is a picture of Ben and I photoshopped on a giant cake (hasty). So I'll make new ones. Or better yet! I'll paste the face of someone else over Ben's (my fish, Elrond).

Ben says he's going to bed and on his way (over his shoulder) asks if I want to have sex. I sigh and splay on the couch like *I'm* tired of *this situation* (not just him, see?). He shrugs and leaves, but I did kind of want to have sex. Which is the problem with thinkers like me, always two steps ahead, but relentlessly alone.

I go to the pantry where I keep a Cheerios box full of plastic grocery bags—hear me out (I do love whales). What are you going to do when it's the end of the world and you find a locker of canned ham or bandaids? Be prepared. Save a few plastic bags (not enough to clog a whale's stomach, mind. I can't stress this enough) and keep them in your pocket after The Big Day happens (The Big Day being the end of the world). Don't tell the cashier why, just say you forgot your canvas bags. I count mine now—six, folded neatly into squares. I check them for holes—none. Make sure the cashier uses bags with *no holes*. If there's a hole, say, I'm really sorry to be *that person*, but can you get a different bag? Then change the subject so the tension doesn't linger.

There's a problem. And I know what you're thinking. How can a person so fully steeped in preparedness feel the worldly weight of problems? It's interesting, because that's what *I thought*. The problem is I'm not sure I can kill a person. And there are plenty of spontaneous crises that could lead to killing (home invasion, dementia, someone trying to *kill me* for my *last can of ham*). I have a knife, it's a paring knife and it's ceramic. I keep it under the mattress, but I'm sure I could never watch someone's eyes go vacant as their life empties onto my carpet, and I'm concerned ceramic will snap in two when it hits bone. I need you to understand, I don't want to kill *anyone*. But *spontaneous crises* are real and you should explore this part of your humanity.

I don't know about God, since only the perceptible is knowable (Karl Marx). This keeps me up at night. Ben believes in God, which is why he has sex guilt and also hope. I keep religious books around the apartment and have memorized key sections from each in preparation for The Big Day (The Big Day being death or the end of the world—save your bags!). What I hope: that God is a kindly man-woman with downy-soft cheeks. What I fear: that God is a vengeful dickhead.

Other than that, I think my life is going quite well. I'm currently recording songs for my future grandson's playlist—songs that hold my memories like a glass holds water. I sing about my mother being a nurse and my dad driving truck and how his arms had thick black hair like a bear. There's a whole verse about throwing up during French class in third grade that I almost took out, but memories are our diaries (Oscar Wilde)—without them we are nothing. I sing about how my favorite snack is banana yogurt and the one I hate most is Peanut Butter M&Ms, and I just added the part where I said no to sex with Ben, but wished I didn't. *He walks from me, with shuffling steps, I was kind of joking but he didn't get it* (to the tune of *Your Song* by Elton John)

I don't think he loves me, but at least I have these:
Flour for cake, and a drawer full of names.

I didn't say I was a good songwriter. I never said that.

Now I curl up next to Ben, he smells good (will I remember?). I count the bumps in his spine. Don't ask me how many there are, I'll add that to my song tomorrow. And, quite frankly, it's private.

Zilla, 2015

by Jeff Somers

The sound of bottles floating in the pool. *Son, she said, have I got a little story for you.*

*

She'd decided that Cliffside was a lot of people's last stop. It wasn't a bad neighborhood, not really; it was close to New York, offered several ways into the city, and bustled respectfully enough. The buildings were worn and wind scarred, the apartments cheap and unrenovated, the tiny groceries on every other corner all smelled like onions. People sat on their front stoops and watched you go about your business, apparently without any business of their own. Kids drove around at night playing loud music that rose and fell outside her window like ocean waves.

The apartment wasn't bad, either. It was five rooms in a line, with floors painted brown and kitchen cabinets that were permanently sticky from decades of other people's cooking, but the water pressure was fine and there was a lot of light, and she'd discovered that she could climb out onto the fire escape in the back and ascend to the roof, where there was something close to open air.

But everything was worn smooth and handled, handed-down and rubbed. None of it was new, all of it was off-center and settled. When she signed the lease and moved her stuff into the place, she knew she was leaning into a decline she'd begun some time before. She'd been in the city, hustling, and now she was outside the city—still hustling, but she'd lost her grip and slid down a few rungs and instead of climbing back up with trembling limbs and sweat stinging her eyes she'd decided to say fuck it and find cheaper rent.

The bodega on the corner was called Pedro's on the faded, weathered sign, but was currently owned by a bearded man of indeterminate ethnicity who seemed to believe he was part of the resistance in some sort of blasted dystopia. When she entered and plucked two plastic bottles of gin from the back shelves, he watched her approach as if preparing to chase her when she ran. As he rang her up, he insisted in musical, accented English that he could get anything she wished, all she had to do was ask and he would track it down for her like he was running a blockade or crossing the front line to bring nylons and cans of sardines back to the trapped city dwellers instead of clicking a mouse or making a phone call.

*

Her neighbors were mostly older folks. The woman downstairs spoke English with an imperious energy that was disconcerting, like she was physically producing words from within herself, spitting them up as physical objects. She had a son who was obviously a challenge, an overgrown body and underdeveloped mind, and she wore the exhausted, deep-eyed look of someone who would die so deeply in sleep debt her body would immediately turn to dust.

The superintendent was a tall, gangly man named Spencer who spent his days acting as if he was single-handedly holding the building together via the magic ritual of polishing everything with a greasy rag. He was nice to her, though she began avoiding him on her second day when he helped her carry some boxes up to her apartment and then stayed for forty minutes telling her the Complete and Total History of the Building According to Spencer, composed of lengthy recitations of names in a biblical rhythm that meant nothing to her.

Up above on the top floor was a shy, quiet Japanese man who was a particular friend of Spencer's. She found his silent, ninja-like movements around the building disconcerting; she always expected to find him lurking in a corner, filming her. He appeared to speak no English and the idea of him thinking Japanese thoughts all the time was equally disturbing. She wondered what in the world he and Spencer did, two old men with no shared language. All her theories were unsavory.

Down below somewhere was the middle-aged white man who favored the sort of shapeless, too-large shirts and trousers exclusive to middle-aged white men, giving them the appearance of having shrunk slightly since getting dressed the day before. He was polite and disinterested in the halls, and looked like a drinker to her jaundiced eye, though she never smelled any liquor on him. His name, according to the mail-box he opened promptly at noon every day as if expecting it to not be empty, was Marks.

The demon who lived above her was also a middle-aged white man, because Cliffside was the sort of neighborhood where the dregs of prior immigrant waves were still clinging to the bottom of everything like barnacles. The first night, when she collapsed in drunken exhaustion onto her mattress, one bottle of gin empty, she enjoyed five minutes of being too head-spinningly tired to sleep before ludicrous jazz music began thumping down from above—and not the sort of tinkly, coffeeshop, jazz-for-people-who-hate-jazz jazz, but the Buddy Rich-on-Speed kind that was all syncopated drums and sweaty, spitty trumpet. The man also wore shoes while walking on his old wood floors, which as far as she was concerned made him a complete, irredeemable monster.

She'd marched wearily upstairs. She was no rookie; this was the seventh apartment she'd rented in her life, if only the second without roommates, and she'd had her share of assholes who imagined they lived in some cocoon of privilege. She banged on the door for five minutes and got no response, so she marched back downstairs and dug through boxes. She found many wondrous treasures, several of which she had no memory of packing. At one point she lifted her old high school yearbook from a box and held it for a few bars of music; it felt warm and alive in her hand. Then she put it down, found some paper, and wrote her upstairs neighbor what she hoped was and intended to be the nastiest note he'd ever received in his life.

*

"Comes from money, Mr. Hammond," Spencer said the next day, working his rag over a random doorknob. He glanced at her. "You're Number Three, right?"

"Zilla," she replied, nodding, making a private bet as to how long it would be before he started calling her *Zill*, a nickname she despised but which followed her like bad luck. It was eleven o'clock in the morning and she was in the process of forcing herself to wait until the afternoon before dismissing her pounding headache and sour stomach with a cocktail. "Money, and he lives *here*?" she asked.

Spencer scoffed. "He ain't *got* money. He comes *from* money, same way I come from Newark."

She accepted this and contemplated a new theory that life was just an immense sorting algorithm, and she had been sorted down to Cliffside Heights, Bergen City, New Jersey.

In the warm afternoon, all the heat below her rising into her apartment, she dozed in a sweat and dreamed of voices raised in alarm, bottles clicking in the pool, that guitar riff, soaring and twisting and already old-fashioned when she'd gotten to it.

*

The war escalated the next evening when the music and the stomping was repeated. She'd been dreaming about Quentin, a recurring dream she'd been having for four years which began with their first kiss, her first ever kiss, timid and weird in a movie theater dark and sticky and he tasted like Southern Comfort and the warm jelly burn in her stomach from the liquor spreading through her veins and bones.

52

Then the scene shifted and they were under water, a thick viscous darkness that was cold and clingy and slimy, the surface up above like a sheet of plate glass. And when she turned to Quentin, sweet, odd little Quent, he was dead, swollen and pale, his skin flaking and peeling just as she imagined it had when they pulled him from the Everglades.

She woke up suffocating as if the air had been sucked from the room. The sound of drums dripped from above, the pulse of a dying, terrified man.

She once again dragged herself up to pound on his door. Then she went down into the basement, where the breaker boxes were lined up on a piece of plywood directly across from the single coin-op washer and dryer. She located #5 and with savage glee she slapped all the breakers over to OFF.

When she got back to her apartment, the quiet was bliss. She worried for a moment about retaliation, then poured herself the last of the second bottle and fell asleep. She didn't see Quentin again.

The quiet held for a few days. She imagined that Hammond was trying to puzzle out what had happened, was perhaps superstitiously keeping his volume low in case it was ghosts, or aliens, or Acts of God. But then she was startled out of a nap by the thunderous roll of snare and clarinet, and she was staggering down the stairs and through the basement door, only to discover the man had locked his breaker box with a padlock. She retrieved the old ballpeen hammer that constituted exactly one-third of her toolbox (the other two-thirds being a rusted flathead screwdriver that served a multitude of purposes and a tape measure that had never actually been used), returned to the basement, and a few seconds later the blessed quiet had returned.

*

She bought two more bottles of gin from Pedro's for fifteen dollars. The price should have concerned her, made her suspect that Not Pedro was distilling his own in the basement from whatever rotting vegetables were left in the dirty bins at the front of the store, but she thought it more prudent to concentrate on the budgetary angle. She'd crunched some numbers and realized that in order to survive the winter with her rent paid she was either going to have to find a much better job or live on approximately five dollars a day, total. This was theoretically possible, but it required that her liquor budget be Pedro-sized.

Back in her surprisingly warm apartment, she set the bottles on the old wooden table that had been left behind along with three chairs, her only pieces of actual furniture. She studied them with red eyes and runny nose. She'd discovered gin twenty years before, at the Outing Party. She could remember George Heffernan, his shirt collar popped, sunglasses on at night, serving her cocktails he called GSTs, for *gin sans tonic*, which were just gin with lemon wedges. They were horrible and terrible and disgusting and she'd consumed about seven, never felt drunk, and had no hangover the next day despite all the horror and awfulness. She'd been chasing the experiment ever since.

Years and years later, George had gotten extremely drunk at a party during a bad snowstorm, and rather than walk home had crawled under everyone's winter coats in the spare bedroom, where he vomited, choking to death under a heavy carpet of Gore-Tex and faux fur. She could still see him at Bishop Carlbus Prep, seashell necklace and Vans, sunglasses propped on his head.

In her youth, during college and her early days in New York as a broke young professional as opposed to a broke middle-aged professional, gin as a drink of choice, as a signature move, felt baller. The proles could have their lite beers, their whiskey sours, their low-class flights of shots. She ordered gin with a twist and smiled at the reactions she imagined. It made her feel unique and interesting.

Her tolerance became part of the legend. She was the cool young girl who drank neat liquor and kept up with the boys. Hangovers were part of the game, comparing your misery, sneaking off at lunch to a bar to get some medicine. Being lightly hammered in the afternoon after being sick in the morning felt naughty, wild. Days went by in bleary, blurry jump cuts. The most recent of which saw her snapping awake in HR, being informed that she was being let go, she would get no severance, she would be escorted from the building as soon as she'd gathered her things.

She'd waited for the elevator, but when several co-workers emerged she'd turned and taken her box of possessions to the stairs. As she turned around each landing, she thought for a split second she could see Amy at the bottom, her head twisted around. She thought she could hear music.

Son, she said, have I got a little story for you.

*

Just as she was beginning to suspect that the smell of onions pervading her apartment would not actually fade away over time—that perhaps it was part of the molecular structure of the place and not just the lingering impression of the previous occupant, which in turn led her to worry over the possibility that she herself was beginning to smell like onions without realizing it, that the smell was getting into her skin, her clothes, her very DNA—the strange Japanese man upstairs died.

She'd begun the day with resolve. Head pounding, stomach churning, she'd decided *this* was the day she planted her feet, caught a branch as it hurtled towards her, and hung on. *This* was the moment when she began the climb back. She might never make the summit she'd once thought within reach, but any gained altitude would be better than the wind in her ears as she plummeted.

She was working at the kitchen table when she noticed the commotion—steps up and down the stairs, doors opening, sirens. She closed her laptop carefully, the left hinge held together with duct tape, and listened at her front door for a moment, trying to ascertain whether she should grab her things and light out the back, shimmying down the fire escape and fleeing into the weeds and junky yards of Bergen City to start a new life as an urchin.

When she crept upstairs, she found paramedics filling out paperwork along with Spencer and Marks, standing in the hallway. They didn't notice her, and Spencer's obvious posture of grief made her retreat without inserting herself, feeling for the first time that perhaps her neighbors were human beings instead of demonic, distorted homunculi placed there solely to torture or amuse her.

This led to her contemplating the fact that if the Japanese man was a real human being, then his death was a warning: She'd been sorted into Bergen City, into Cliffside, into this apartment building, and if it was her final destination and not simply a step on her way to the bottom, then she had to seriously consider the possibility that she was going to die there.

After all, she was the last one alive. Victor Drummond had been pushed under an oncoming subway the same day she'd been fired.

She poured herself a stiff drink and didn't bother chopping up any lemons. Later, so drunk typing a single word into a search engine took two minutes, she found the song and played it on repeat until she passed out.

*

She made her living as a transcriptionist. It was all freelance, all over the Internet. She downloaded videos and audio files, she listened to them, she typed up the words. It was the sort of job any monkey could do, and she felt ridiculous doing it. She had a degree in Communications. She'd gotten good grades. She'd worked for advertising agencies, she'd had people report to her.

But that was the thing about the city. It spun you around, and if you didn't hang on you lost your grip and started hitting things on the way down.

The fact that it wasn't complicated work didn't mean it was easy. It was, actually, quite difficult. The audio was usually muddy and very difficult to parse. She slowed it down and looped it, sometimes sitting for long moments with her eyes closed, listening to the same incomprehensible blast of audio over and over again, a second's worth of speech that had turned into a blob of noise because of a passing bus, a cough, or an accent.

The hourly pay was terrible, so she cheated industriously. She created three distinct freelance identities and took on more jobs than were technically possible, then did Internet searches to see if the audio had already been transcribed, which sometimes happened with videos that had already lived online for a while. She then extracted the audio and uploaded it to a free machine transcription site, which spat back garbled, terrible text files, but this at least gave her something to work with. Then she aggressively guessed and sometimes made up entire sentences from whole cloth. As she sank lower the proportion of bullshit in her transcriptions grew, but no one ever called her out on it.

*

The sorting had begun, she realized, eight years ago. She'd still been at her first job out of school, comfortably writing copy as part of a small team. Then she'd been downsized. She'd dutifully refreshed her resume and set up interviews, and was pleasantly surprised to find she was relatively popular among hiring managers, all of whom saw great things for her.

One, a brusque middle-aged woman who leaned back in her chair with her resume held aloft as if seeking invisible ink messages on the thick, creamy paper, told her that she would, of course, have to take on a manager's role at her age and her level of experience. She remembered vividly the air of received wisdom with which this was communicated, the matter-of-factness of the statement impressing her. Two weeks later she started a new job that came with four people reporting to her. She'd arrived on her first day in a new suit, carrying a new briefcase. She felt grown-up. She remembered because it was the day she'd heard that Desmond Brady, who'd once asked her to dance with him at a school social and who she'd seen from time to time on television in small acting roles, and once in a fast food commercial eating hamburgers like his life depended on it, had been thrown from a snowmobile and killed.

Just a month later, she knew she'd made a terrible mistake.

Some people, she thought, were born for management. They somehow effortlessly compelled others to do their jobs while dealing with paperwork, their own work, and the many headaches of managing human resources. Zilla found it confusing and dispiriting. Two of her direct reports thought they should have been promoted, and treated her every decision as the mistake of a rank amateur. Deadlines slipped, details were missed, and within six months she'd found herself having regular check-ins with her own boss, who greeted her every statement with a pinched expression of doubt.

Panicked, she fled. And then fled again. Slowly, her options constricted and she began to wonder if she'd always been secretly incompetent, if her sheen of professional success had always been an illusion. When she was fired from her last job, the firing that had finally pushed her out of New York and sent her drifting downward to a five-room railroad apartment in Cliffside Heights, Bergen City, New Jersey, she'd felt something akin to relief instead of despair.

*

After sprinting from that first management job and settling on a course that led to Bergen City, she became obsessed with the social media of old friends, colleagues, relatives, and complete strangers, all of whom had better careers. Her old high school friends especially seemed to be charmed; short weirdo Leo Barone looked like a millionaire, working in finance. Una, as thin as ever, opened a trendy art gallery in the City. Kate Huxtable was an executive at a top insurance company, her Instagram a parade of amazing hair styles and new frocks. She had no idea what Ernest Bundy did for a living, but he seemed to always be on vacation somewhere, and Fanny Heck did nothing but volunteer in exotic places, implying a lavish income.

She knew their stories by heart. Leo swallowed thumbtacks that had been dropped into his shawarma, and they'd perforated his bowels. Una fell into an old, forgotten drain pipe, broke both legs, and died of exposure before they'd found her. Kate was chopped up with an axe and left by the side of her Tesla on a deserted country road. Ernest inhaled a peach pit and died in an ice cream parlor in front of his three kids, his face turning purple.

She knew, on one level, that she'd been one of the Poor Kids at Bishop Carlbus Prep. A scholarship kid. Out of twenty-six kids in the Senior Class, there had been three of them on scholarship, the rest were rich, ranging from merely wealthy to Illuminati-scale rich. So it wasn't a fair comparison. Fanny Heck didn't *have* to work.

But she knew better. Whatever advantages the other kids had, they were *killing it*. They were being promoted, being taken seriously, moving upwards. At least they had been before they all died. If she was never going to have the access they had, she could have at least paralleled their success on a different, lower track. Instead, she'd boofed on the fifty-yard line.

Even though it was painful and horrifying, she couldn't stop herself from following along with them all. Every promotion, every new house, every baby. And it made her sick, and when she noticed how many of them were dead, she felt better. Then, worse.

She thought she detected the pattern, finally. She began searching for the obituaries. At night she heard the bottles, and the guitar riff, and saw Amy Keaton's face staring up at her from the basement floor.

*

Sometimes, late at night when she was being especially creative with her assignments, interpreting muddy monologues as epic speeches about man's duty to a universe of random chance and increasing entropy, she contemplated the likely possibility that Cliffside Heights and the yellow brick building were not her final resting place in the existential sorting machine, but simply a plateau where she would idle away a few months or years before being tipped down to the next level.

The freelance would dry up. She would get sick and have no insurance. She would miss two, three, four months rent, and be evicted.

Or the freelance would hold steady, allowing her to hang on by her fingernails until she was the weird old lady in #3, and one day she would be found dead in her bathtub, a neighbor drawn by the smell, the eerie silence, and no one would have the energy or impetus to figure out if it had been suicide or simple despair. She contemplated the other ways her classmates had expired: Amy Keaton, fell down the stairs, broke her neck. Lived for some hours, alone, unconscious and possibly paralyzed. Hector Ricardo, mugged and beaten to death. Nothing was stolen. James Forman took lye in an apparent accident involving a dietary supplement. Yoric Evans was hit over the head with a piece of sculpture during a break-in at his apartment. Titus Cunningham, Rhoda Anderson, Ida Tanner, Desmond Brady, Winnie Taylor, Prue Nelson, and Basil Jefferson. Explosion, fire, drowning, thrown from a snowmobile, accidentally locked inside a walk-in freezer overnight, trampled, killed by bear during a camping trip with his Boy Scout troop. The Sandford twins, Quentin sunk into a mire, his sister Olive stabbed repeatedly with a rusty old awl at their family home. Susan Petrie, who crashed her car when she had a seizure on the freeway. Bluth, Huang, Heffernan, Bundy. Drowned, natural causes despite a clean bill of health, smothered, choking. Clair Addams and Xerc Bartokomous, anorexia and *mice*. Fanny Heck, extreme anemia from leeches she encountered while serving as a missionary in Africa.

She thought drinking herself to death at least sounded purposeful.

She sipped gin and tapped her fingers to the beat of Mr. Hammond's music, pounding down from above, pushing her under.

*

At the age of thirteen, as her parents went through what turned out to be a long and bitter divorce that might not even be entirely over, as far as she knew, twenty-five years and both their deaths later, Zilla began experiencing Exploding Head Syndrome.

It didn't happen every night. Sometimes three or four times a week, sometimes once a month, but for years she was semi-regularly awakened at night by an incredibly loud, terrifying bang that sounded like her house collapsing around her. But then she would sit up in bed, soaked with sweat, trembling, listening to the suffocating hiss of the fan, the drip of the bathroom faucet, and, later on in the infinite process of the divorce, possibly her father's thunderous snoring.

She never told her parents, who had demonstrated a disturbingly itchy trigger finger when it came to her mental health. She diagnosed herself with an Internet search and some videos. There was no cure. There was not even an official disease, despite the millions of hits she found.

It reached crisis levels in her Junior Year of high school. She lost so much sleep huge black bags formed under her eyes and her grades fell. The explosions that sent her, rigid and damp, hurtling from sleep sounded like an atomic bomb going off in the next room, and the sudden, perfect silence that followed was just as horrifying. Going back to sleep was impossible, so she found herself roaming her room with headphones, exhausted and bored.

She had her first drink at Prudence Nelson's house, red wine stolen from her parents' cellar, where there were so many bottles they'd never notice one or three missing. They'd gotten silly and sloppy, and then she'd dozed off on Prue's couch. She woke up with a headache and sketchy stomach, but she realized she'd slept for almost three hours without hearing a thing.

Zilla flipped blearily through the yearbook and thought incredulously that this had been her high-water mark. Senior Year at Bishop Carlbus Prep, until the After the Outing Party and Amy Keaton's death, had been the literal best year of her life. This was so utterly basic and cliche she was offended. But it was undeniable. With her nights peaceful, with her parents in a momentary holding pattern that she recalled as Truce Mark One, with her class at BCP winnowed down to twenty-six kids with whom she had a passing familiarity if not an intimate relationship, things were calm. She was able to think. Catch her breath.

She stared down at Amy Keaton's photo. Her face, fat and round and squinting distrustfully at the camera, reminded her what a total bitch Amy had been. Loud. Bullying. Always angry, always disappointed. Always *easily* disappointed.

The head explosions had started again after the Outing Party. Except, instead of explosions, she started waking up to the sound of Amy Keaton screaming in her ear.

She threw up a lot, but it wasn't so bad. When she'd been younger she'd had a morbid fear of puking, and she'd put a lot of effort into avoiding the experience. But now she did it frequently, and didn't mind—it was a relief, a pleasure. She began to feel poorly, but all it took was a quick trip to the bathroom and she was ready to have another drink and get back to work.

She took a creative spin in her transcription services, crafting sentences and even whole paragraphs from an artistic understanding of the subject matter and the speaking style without the benefit of actually listening closely to the recordings. Superstitiously, she continued to play the recordings as she wrote, she just didn't pay any attention to them.

Surprisingly, no one complained. She kept snagging assignments, and being able to make up most of the text made it go much faster.

When she came across someone's obituary, she opened the yearbook and put a thick red X over their photo, along with a date. It made her feel better, for a moment. Then it made her want another drink. And another drink made her remember the bottles floating in the pool. The braying laughter coming from the living room in that huge, cold house. The throbbing music. And the sudden silence and then the crowd of bodies, overheated, pushing for a view.

And Amy. Staring up at them, as if in on the joke, but unamused.

*

The war with Hammond turned into a cold war that ruined her sleep. He spent some money on a real lock, and no matter how she pounded away at it, squinting in the gloom of the basement as it dodged and ducked away from her, gin singing in her veins, it held. Every time she managed to drink herself into a fitful slumber, a spray of snare and bass, trumpet blast and clarinet call would drag her back. It was worse than the explosions, in a way.

She would drag herself from the bed and get up on top of a chair to hammer at the ceiling. She shouted. The mystery of why no one else complained, why everyone else seemed able to ignore not just Hammond's boozy jazz concerts but also her own screaming into the abyss that *was* Hammond's boozy jazz concerts was inscrutable. She wondered if she was dead, if she'd slipped off the edge one evening, rolled out of bed insensibly drunk and cracked her head on the edge of the frame and bled out, and this was her gasping Owl Creek Bridge moment.

She rejected the idea for one simple reason: Not enough ghosts.

*

She thought of Prudence, who'd been dead two years before she heard about it. She imagined her, crushed under the weight of bodies, merciless steel-toed boots and stiletto heels and crushed fingers her final sensations. There was, she knew, no dignity in death. Everyone died badly. But Prue had died worse than some. She sometimes wondered what had brought Prue into that bar, in a small town, apparently alone.

Twenty-five people under the age of 45, two-and-a-half-decades of bad deaths. Twenty five pictures in her yearbook with a thick red X over their faces. And then her own photo, beaming back at the camera, the photo taken weeks before the Outing Party, when everything had been wonderful. She wore her hair up, her mother's cat necklace, a simple black dress. She looked young and fresh. She had great teeth. She'd always been oddly proud of her teeth, which had erupted inside her mouth perfect without any dentist's intervention.

The page before the Senior Photos was a spread devoted to the Senior Outing. She remembered how exciting the Outing sounded to her when the older kids described it, all the Seniors and Juniors talking like past Senior Outings had been transformative, spectacular, possibly illegal. Lives had been changed, virginities lost, fortunes made on past Senior Outings. Among her tiny, insular class, shrinking over the course of four years from forty-three kids to twenty-six, the Outing had taken on an occult aspect. Rumors involved international trips, elaborate character-building alternate reality games, survival challenges—the only thing everyone was certain about was the awesomeness of the Outing.

But the Outing was just a retreat. They were piled onto a bus, driven to a campground, and for two days they got a lot of bullshit group therapy. Their phones and devices were taken away, they were encouraged to roam the grounds, and at night they were gathered around a campfire to engage in various weird chants and confessions. And the morning of the third day as they hastily packed their shit back onto the bus, they were solemnly warned to never reveal what they'd experienced, in order to preserve the surprise for the next class.

That night, as was traditional, there was an After the Outing Party. Amy Keaton hosted, because her parents were away and it was just her and her little brother Alton.

Zilla remembered the bottles floating in the pool. She remembered Amy raging, pissed off that no one was paying attention to her party rules.

She remembered Amy's scream. Everyone rushing to the basement door. Amy staring up at them from the bottom of the stairs.

She remembered a moment of shocked silence. And then the guitar riff blasting from the stereo, the perfect song, the *ideal* song for the moment you discover your classmate and party host has fallen down a flight of stairs in a stupor and broken her neck.

Son, she said, have I got a little story for you.

*

Over the course of four years at Bishop Carlbus Prep, Zilla had gained a shadow education in BCP lore and myths.

For example, she knew that the second-most important Senior Outing party dated back forty years or so, and was enshrined in the June 5th issue of the Bergen Journal as a report about a raucous party that resulted in Mr. and Mrs. Steven Douglas being arrested on charges of supplying minors with liquor. The legendary status of this party began with lurid tales of the parents working as bartenders for their children and their schoolmates and includes, in the most recent tellings, intimations that Mrs. Douglas, an attractive older woman of some distinction, being quite drunkenly free with several of the kids. The fact that this party made the papers in an era when the *papers* were the Internet made it a very important piece of BCP folklore no matter how old the story gets. Every incoming Freshman class heard a version of the legend.

Zilla knew that the *most* important Senior Outing party, however, would forever be the Seaver Shit Party.

Brett Seaver was a Big Man on BCP's campus, and his photo and several trophies still adorn the awards case in the lobby of the BCP building. He still held a few records for the BCP in the track and field category; BCP was too small for team sports. He was, if you dig up his yearbook photo, a good-looking kid, great bone structure, really fit, an easy smile. He was popular and off to Stanford and did not host the Senior Outing Party that year. He did, however, shit his pants during it.

As the story goes, Brett was actually a ball of quivering stress. He'd cheated industriously through BCP, knew basically nothing, and, worse, *knew* he was an idiot. His acceptance to Stanford—he hadn't written the essay himself—filled him with so much unease he stopped sleeping.

He told no one. He affected to be the same laid-back kid who never wore socks. But inside he was a mess, and self-medicated using whatever he could steal from his parents' medicine cabinet. At the Senior Outing Party, he parked himself by the pool with a bottle of Jack Daniels, a pack of cigarettes, and a pair of sunglasses, and proceeded to drink, smoke, or eat anything he was handed. He slipped into a near-total nervous system shutdown, passed out, and shit his pants. A fact discovered some time later when the party had mellowed out and slow jams were tinkling in the night and several virginities were being lost in the upstairs bedrooms, and someone remarked on the smell.

The night that Brett Seaver shit his pants was immediately codified as the greatest party anyone had ever attended. It became a part of BCP jargon. The Masons had *are you a traveling man* and the BCP had *well, that was great but it was no Seaver Shit Party, was it*?

Zilla remembered that the Keaton Party was earmarked for legendary status from the beginning. No parents in sight, the end of the school year looming, the Outing—it was all a recipe for greatness. She could remember the palpable sense of excitement. People talked about it as if the world would be forever changed in its aftermath. She could remember walking the halls of the BCP and hearing it spoken of in dewy tones of awe: The Keaton Party, After the Outing. All in Implied Caps, like some sort of historic event.

Amy was red hot for the party to be epic, but Zilla remembered Amy as red hot for everything. For weeks, plans were laid. Liquor, wine, and beer were acquired through various means including older siblings, sketchy neighbors, unmonitored home supplies, and outright theft. People pledged to bring weed, pills stolen from medicine cabinets, and an exotic list of other pharma, most of which was known to be fanciful but still ignited visions of a bacchanalia unlike any previous Senior Class had ever managed.

The Keaton House was more of a compound. There was the main house, six bedrooms and seven baths, everything too large, too far apart. Changing a light bulb required a work order and construction permits because the sconces were so high up. There was a four-car garage and a mother-in-law unit which was essentially a small cottage, plus a large shed in the backyard. There was a pool and a finished basement with a wet bar, as well.

Only a handful of students had ever been to the Keaton House. Zilla recalled that the Keatons didn't approve of kids. They regarded them as barely housebroken chaos agents who had no respect for property or appreciation for the time and effort they'd put into the design and decoration of the home they spent a maximum of seventy-four days in every year. The place was like a museum; there were entire rooms no one was allowed to actually use, and even in the common areas there were chairs or other features that Mrs. Keaton had clearly marked as untouchable.

In fact, the square footage of the Keaton Compound that was off-limits to everyone but highly-trained professionals from various fields including but not limited to catering, cleaning, security, and interior design grew at a rate that threatened to engulf nearby homes within a few short years.

*

The audio recordings she downloaded from her transcription clients got muddier and muddier, the words slurring into a wall of noise. Occasionally a word would rise to the surface as she sat there sipping her GSTSL, a new variation of her favorite cocktail now sans tonic *and* lemons, but mainly it was static and noise and she began writing a lengthy epic novel in short bursts of ersatz transcription.

When her login credentials stopped working, she realized it had been some time since she'd been paid for the work.

She busied herself with collecting information about her dead classmates, sitting on the bed with her laptop and the yearbook, bopping along with puffy eyes and labored breathing to the lurching rhythms beating down from above. She imagined she would write a book about them, chronicling their deaths, something moving and revelatory. She knew this would mean discussing and revealing what had happened to Amy, but she realized she was okay with this. It would be necessary, for one thing, and for another it didn't matter. They were all dead, except her, and she knew she couldn't last long.

It would be a relief.

Head spinning, breathing feeling like entirely too much trouble, she roamed the apartment glass in hand, breaking into little spins and balletic moves as the beat went on from above. Then she would sail back to the bed and spill gin and push the soggy clippings and notes around and flip through the yearbook.

And then she paused, going quiet, the emptiness filled by a sudden crash of snare and cymbal muted by the ceiling. She realized she'd seen something, something in a dream, or maybe in real life, something long ago but quite recently. A dark figure, a tall, spectral figure in a heavy overcoat and a fancy hat, looming over each of them. She'd seen it, she'd seen *him*, Death, visiting each of them. When Rhoda had burned alive in the bathroom of her apartment, he'd been there in the mirror, grinning. When Fanny drank water infested with leeches in Africa and they attached themselves to her throat and bled her to death, he'd been there, a black umbrella shielding his face from the hot sun. When Zerc contracted hantavirus from airborne particles of mouse shit, he was visited, she was sure, by this looming figure in his hospital bed as his insides turned to liquid and breathing became the same as drowning, she was sure of it.

As she poured the last of the bottle into her glass she felt a warm sense of completion. She'd finally cracked the code. She'd finally understood. She was part of something enormous, and inevitable.

*

It was Hector who switched the music. This Zilla remembered clearly.

Amy originally scored the party to a sludge of pop hits and dance slurry, constant basslines that made your teeth ache and your eyeballs dance. But then Hector Ricardo and Ernest Bundy arrived with their guitars and portable amps and began setting them up in the formal living room—despite Amy's immediate and profane complaints—so their excruciatingly, almost aggressively terrible mathcore band *Polybius* could perform the four songs they'd composed. And Amy had lost. her. shit.

Amy Keaton losing her shit wasn't unusual, of course. Amy lost her shit constantly. Amy's default setting was SHIT:LOST. Everyone knew that the After the Outing Party at the Keaton compound was going to be a prime-time Amy Shit Losing Moment; that had been part of the fun, happily lapping up all of Amy's rules and regulations about the party with the sure knowledge that everyone would ignore her, making her ragey.

Ragey Amy was very popular.

Zilla remembered the escalation. The painter's tape across doorways torn down. The stolen diet chocolate bars passed out to everyone. The invasion of the master bedroom and bath. Throwing bottles into the pool and laughing.

And Amy raging, raging, raging.

Zilla remembered the shouts and screams. She remembered being very, very drunk. She remembered feeling weirdly unsafe. They carried all the televisions out to the patio and began searching the house for extension cords. When they discovered the door to the basement was locked, Basil Jefferson, who would one day in the future be mauled by a bear, took off his shirt and hurled himself against it until it snapped open, sending Basil crashing into the opposite wall hard enough to crack the plaster.

She remembered kids on the roof overlooking the patio, dancing. She remembered Amy, red faced and crying, screaming that she was going to cut the fucking power if Hec and Ernie played one single fucking goddamned power chord, and she remembered the silence as Hector stopped tuning up to shout at her. She remembered Amy standing at the top of the basement stairs to marvel at the cracked plaster, her rage reaching incandescent levels as a red glow began to leak out of the cracks in her skin. She remembered Amy stopping and turning to shout back at Hector.

And then Amy went down the stairs.

Zilla remembered the strange silence that followed. The sound of everyone moving at once to crowd around the doorway. Bleary and blurry, amazed. She remembered Amy at the bottom of the stairs, looking back up at them, her head twisted in a way it shouldn't be twisted.

There was a beat of silence. Two.

And then the stereo, loaded up by a spiteful Hector. That guitar riff, forever seared into her mind.

Son, she said, have I got a little story for you.

*

She woke up in the hall at the foot of the landing, one arm draped on the bottom step leading up to the floor above. She stared around blearily, working her mouth, wincing as she moved her shoulder and was rewarded with a sharp stab of pain. The sound of drums drooled down from above, a thick cloud of percussion that sank down like smog, smothering her in heavy bass.

She rolled over onto her knees, head pounding. She pulled herself onto her feet with laborious effort, fought back a wave of nausea, and hung onto the banister for support. She rifled back through her memories for clues as to how she'd wound up in the hallway and found nothing going back some time, just empty blankness. Smoothing her clothes and shaking herself, she staggered back towards the open door of her own apartment.

In the bathroom, she didn't have to kneel down and throw her arms around the toilet like an amateur. She'd perfected the art of simply bending over and throwing up, a stream of clear liquid, pinkish when it hit the water. This was followed by cramps, and she remained bent over the toilet for some time, breathing hard and humming as her guts spasmed.

Sweating, she walked unsteadily into the kitchen and found the plastic jug of gin. She swallowed some, then took another swig and rinsed her mouth out. She felt better, and everything clarified.

For a moment she just stood there studying the mess of papers and photos on the kitchen table. Ancient artifacts, mementos of her high school days. Standing in Cliffside in her railroad apartment, she couldn't believe she'd once attended a pricey private school, that she'd once dreamed of being a superstar, a Draperesque force of nature ramming corporate America's wretched things down everyone's collective throat, a master of the universe. That scholarship had once seemed like her ticket to riches and fortune.

She couldn't believe she'd watched Amy Keaton die. She couldn't believe she was the last one standing. Picking up her laptop, she stared at Victor Drummond's obituary beaming out misery and death. They'd used his high school photo. They always did, she'd noticed, for some reason. Every obituary she'd found for a classmate showed them when they were eighteen—except for Desmond, who'd been sixteen when he graduated—bright and young and shiny.

The truth she'd discovered was obvious: They'd all died at the After the Outing Party. The rest of it had been a spasm, a twitching remnant of life, brain cells dying and firing their last spluttering energy into the void.

The drums pounded from above. They'd lost their jazzy raggedness and become insistent, regular, compulsory. She picked up a random glass and sipped from it, swaying back and forth.

They were dead. *She* was dead. It was the only explanation.

*

They'd danced. For years she'd told herself that she hadn't really believed Amy was dead—it was all just *hilarious*. They were all loaded, and Amy had been such a bitch—the music had dropped as if on cue and it was perfect, so they'd all turned away from the basement door and danced and sang along even though the song itself was terrible, a grinding dirge from a prior age when people like their parents had not yet discovered pop hooks and spat rhymes and good taste. And she told herself that she'd expected Amy to come crawling back upstairs at any moment, foul-mouthed and red-faced. They were kids. They didn't *die*. Dying was for olds.

Then they'd panicked.

The music faded and the drugs wore off and everyone got scratchy-eyed and sore throated and Amy remained at the bottom of the stairs, dead as could fucking be, and they all saw their futures: Ruined, in the main. No one knew or could find out how accurate a time-of-death determination from a medical examiner was, but once the thought was put out there that maybe—just maybe—there was a way to figure out that they'd left her lying there and danced and drank and made out for several hours, there was no dispelling the panic. It would be discovered.

So they'd cleaned up.

*

She realized she was dancing in the hallway. Her apartment door was wide open, light and heat pouring out of it like a portal to the sun. Her head spun, dizzy and light-filled. Hammond's music had gotten to her. It was in her blood, in her ligaments, invisible strings to make her sway and jerk, something dissolved and bonding with gun and red cells to create a new kind of energy.

It was so hot. Sweat dripped off of her. Her heart was pounding. The drums beat.

Snare. Cymbals. Tom. Bass.

She started walking up the stairs. *snare. cymbals. tom. bass.* Each step felt like it was a mile high, and she kept both arms wrapped around the railing as she moved. *snare. cymbals. tom. bass.* She couldn't breathe enough. *have I got a little story for you.* they fished all the bottles from the pool. *snare. cymbals. tom. bass.* they scrubbed the bathrooms. *have I got a little story for you.* they mopped and vacuumed the floors. *snare. cymbals. tom. bass.* they carted off all the liquor and the pills and the hash and the powder. *have I got a little story for you.* they sprayed deodorizers into the air with abandon. *snare. cymbals. tom. bass.* they went home and said nothing. *have I got a little story for you.* the party had never happened. *snare. cymbals. tom. bass.* no one had ever been there.

The upstairs hallway was undulating, rippling with the sonic impact of each drum hit; walking down it was like riding dry, dusty waves. Hammond's door was open, too, but instead of heat and light it was darkness and cold, a purplish glow leaking out. It felt good, splashing against her hot skin with every beat as she crawled closer.

When Amy's parents came home two days later, they found her, swollen and gnawed upon. The twenty-six members of the graduating class of Bishop Carlbus Prep evinced shock and dismay. Surprise and horror.

Hammond's kitchen was exactly like hers, but shrouded in darkness and mystery. The music was no louder, it was still syrupy and thick and pounding. She pulled herself up to the table and lifted a glass. It was the heaviest thing she'd ever picked up, and trembled in her hand. She put it to her lips and tipped backwards, falling and falling and falling.

She panicked, suddenly, the absence of gravity sending a thrill of terror through her. She tried to scream for help, but the drums drowned her out. *My name is Zilla!* she tried to shout. Then, more quietly.

My name is Zilla, she whispered. *And I drank too much gin.*

Grief, Furniture

by Beth Bilderback

This couch is comma-shaped and covered in rich green fabric. Its cushions are stiff and springy, causing a cell phone tossed casually to bounce several inches. This couch required the exertion of two large men to wrestle it into our tiny house, and will never leave it again unless I knock down a wall or two. Not many have sat on it yet—my father, sinking down with an old man's "Oy;" my teenaged son, stretching out to see if it can hold his full length (it can), my son's new girlfriend and her mother, perched awkwardly on the edge while I try in vain to extract conversation from them.

This couch was made for grownups, vintage grownups of the 1930s, cinch-waisted female grownups and men who wore hats and drank martinis. Then it landed with the second generation of the family, beginning another life with my sister's in laws, who decided it would live in a very large wood paneled room, facing two corn-colored armchairs, in a house ruled by collies named Mac, and later, poodles named Mister.

Thirty years later, the last relative leaves, unwillingly, to calcify in assisted living, never knowing the house is being cleared out and sold. This couch moved out of its dank living room to a sunny upholstery shop where it spent two weeks being reinvigorated, like Dorothy in the Emerald City, becoming the color of Emerald City, losing the forlorn moldy smell of its former life, but not the ghosts of the many rumps that sank down upon it.

This couch is not like that couch, the old gray green one, the first I'd ever bought after a lifetime of sad futons, from a Haggerty's salesman named Kwame who wore expensive shoes. That couch was so soft you wanted to pet it, but began sagging in the middle and required propping up with wooden blocks, that couch was where I spent seven years of Saturday nights talking to my boyfriend, the tall, pale boyfriend who, if I am being truthful, bought me the couch himself, and who is gone now, gone like smoke, though not gone like the couch, which was carted out the door by thrift store volunteers, one of whom mentions he used to own the very same couch, the couch with which he started his marriage. The boyfriend left of his own accord, after a short conversation on the couch, and then a long hug, which should have spoken volumes, but did not.

This couch will get to know my sleeping body, a room away from my bed, fraught with insomnia, new territory where I might finally rest without waking every few hours, a clean slate, a patch of grass in a quiet forest, a rivulet running over stones, a long drink of water, dreamless, peaceful.

I Sent an Opossum to Preschool Instead of My Son and No One Noticed

by Steve Edwards

Last fall, after much consideration, my wife and I decided that we could no longer send our son to Sunshine Meadows Preschool. Their recommendation that we hire a full-time developmental aide to help our son "access the Sunshine Meadows Preschool academic curriculum," as well as their thinly veiled insinuations about Autism Spectrum Disorder, weighed upon our decision. But our main reason for pulling our son from the preschool was that we believed the staff should have noticed that for the entire month of October we had been sending an opossum in his place.

We don't believe our son needs the aide the school so firmly requested, and whether he is on the autism spectrum remains to be seen. The suggestion that we ought to "fast-track" him into a diagnosis struck an off-chord with us. Autistic kids deserve a real childhood—not just constant therapy.

So one night in September, in frustration, I said to my wife: "They're dehumanizing him. We could send an opossum in his place and they wouldn't even notice." And we did. We sent an opossum.

It was relatively easy to catch one: an entire family of the varmints live in our trash bin out back. I simply scooped one up, dressed it in one of my son's striped polo shirts and sent it off to school with a backpack and water bottle. In hindsight, I realize this was an incredibly passive-aggressive move, and I regret that. I do. We didn't really think the staff at Sunshine Meadows Preschool wouldn't notice that we had sent a pink-nosed opossum in our son's place. We were just trying to make a point. Our son is more than whatever symptoms one may or may not observe in him.

That first morning we waited for over two hours for a call from Sunshine Meadows. "You sent an opossum to school instead of your son," we imagined someone saying. To our shock and chagrin, we heard nothing.

At pickup that afternoon, my wife asked his teacher if our son seemed at all *off*. His teacher stated that he was a little more tired than usual but had had fun digging in the sandbox all afternoon. While we appreciated his teacher's observation that the nocturnal marsupial we had sent in place of our son seemed "tired," we thought, frankly, she should have realized it was an opossum. The poor fit of the backpack might have clued her in. Also, it wasn't wearing pants. Also, it was an opossum.

As any sensible parents would, we immediately enrolled our son at a new preschool. But we were curious. Would Sunshine Meadows ever finally put two and two together? We sent the opossum the next day, and again the next, and the next, and it just sort of snowballed from there. I'll admit, yes, I began to enjoy the routine and companionship that taking care of an opossum provided, and I missed the little guy while I was at work. I looked forward to the daily reports in the opossum's notebook, which were quite positive. *He sure gobbled down his carrot sticks today!*

Still, regardless of my feelings for the opossum, the troubling fact was that Sunshine Meadows continued to miss the obvious—for weeks. And though I shouldn't have been terribly surprised when pictures of the opossum appeared on the school's newly updated website, it did catch me off guard. No one noticed that on Pirate Day the child in the eye-patch and chewing the corner of his treasure map was actually an opossum? No one thought it strange during Music Hour that one of the children had climbed *inside* the guitar and started hissing and baring its teeth when the janitor tried to remove it? And the picture of the rainbow on the "About Us" page— the giant rainbow the children made by dipping their hands and feet into pans of paint and stamping them all over a gigantic sheet of paper: one can see, plain as day, the opossum's distinctive hind track and the skidding drag marks from its rat-like, semi-prehensile tail.

Now don't get me wrong—my wife and I appreciate that the staff at Sunshine Meadows make a concerted effort to look beyond a child's idiosyncrasies. It was one of the things that originally drew us to Sunshine Meadows. Our son, like all children, has his idiosyncrasies. But just as those idiosyncrasies should not be grounds for robbing him of a childhood, neither should they be excuses for unacceptable behavior.

Imagine an opossum. The teeth, the tail, *the smell.* You can't tell me that no one noticed or remarked upon the horrid stink exuded from the opossum's scent marking glands. Trust me, you would notice.

If our son truly smelled like that we would have expected a call home demanding we bathe him more regularly.

Again, we heard nothing.

Instead of honest communication about his behavior or hygiene, Sunshine Meadows continued to soft-pedal an autism diagnosis by talking about how happy our son seemed at school, how much he smiled. Which, yes: because opossums have mouths full of sharp teeth and, lacking sweat glands, pant like dogs.

But now I'm starting to digress and repeat myself, so let me just sum it up: if our son is on the autism spectrum, my wife and I are prepared to take that journey. We love our son to no end, and we love him unconditionally. We just don't believe that a preschool should ever be in the business of diagnosing children with autism, ADHD, Sensory Processing Disorder, or whatever is currently in vogue.

We also don't believe they should be diagnosing opossums.

I am afraid that if Sunshine Meadows continues to make an issue of the opossum's need for a developmental aide—if they present us with an ultimatum, get the aide or go—we may have to pull the opossum from school. This wouldn't pose such a hardship if we weren't sure that most preschools would indeed notice the fact of its opossum-ness. Yes, of course, I could always return it to the trash bin. I've thought of that. But like I said, I've grown fond of the little stinker. In the mornings at breakfast it curls around my neck and begs bites of my scrambled eggs. I don't know. We're at a crossroads. I guess what breaks my heart, if I'm being honest, is that he *does* seem happy at Sunshine Meadows. I mean, it's not a terrible place for semi-feral pets to spend their days.

"I Sent an Opossum to Preschool" originally appeared in *The Good Men Project*.

Hidden in the Bone

by Jim Krosschell

Lately, as I've progressed from little walks around the living room to real walks around the block, the neighborhood seems to be different. I don't mean the houses, or the hope of approaching spring, or the everlasting trees. I mean you passersby, although I doubt you've changed from a couple of weeks ago. I'm the one seeing things in a new light. I'm the one that's changed, not that you'd notice from the outside. You can't see the little incisions on my belly, or the pad in my pants. Just as I can't see what's going on inside you, the pain in your back, the apostasy of your son, your impending bankruptcy.

You probably keep your stoic face on in public, not giving much away, carefully hiding intelligence or emotion or embarrassment, and if you occasionally smile at a baby in a carriage or frown at an idiot blowing his car horn, it's a measured response, not meant to engage or provoke. I've rarely thought about this, being generally more interested in nature than in people. But now, now that I have my own secret homunculus, a cancerous prostate whose excision may not have been entirely curative, I look at your facade with new sympathy. I wonder what's going on beneath.

It's good that we keep our secrets hidden. Can you imagine the chaos on the streets if we didn't, if we were mastered by our environment like the littlest of animals? Merely sitting on a fence, a sparrow twitches, jerks, and startles as if it were being electro-shocked for insanity. A squirrel in the balsam chatters crazily and fluffs its tail and displaces its head so suddenly that I marvel at the physics. A human is not so maneuverable, or freely responsive; indeed, our depressions and cancers so madly expressed would make our neighborhoods uninhabitable, what with the resulting hernias and concussions and fistfights in the coffee shops.

We big animals, we meat-eaters, can't be acting out at every provocation. We must dissemble. We hide our troubles, we conserve our energy, we wait for prey, we scratch and stretch, we conquer much more than are conquered. The lion, to take the obvious example, is famous for imperturbable lolling. But even the littler carnivores, still a distance from the top of the food chain, display a breath-taking nonchalance. I once watched, for two hours on a December morning in Maine, a fox lying almost motionless on warm rocks at the edge of my yard. It assumed it was safe in the sun. How simple, even joyous, life is when the belly is full, when pain ebbs, and when, in the higher reaches of consciousness, the human mind holds out hope for the future. And if none of these apply, when pain gnaws on emptiness, when things go wrong, the natural response is to strike out with claw or knife to slash and satisfy. The blood gets up. Except that most humans don't succumb. Most of us don't turn warm-bloodedness into hot-headedness.

So we don't often punch the walls or beat the kids. In the progress to civilization, fight or flight has been bred out of our genes. We survive now by buttoning up, walking out our days in patient and beguiling decorum. But is evolutionary advantage all that rewarding? What have we lost by conducting our tantrums in private?

When things go wrong … Maybe that's the clue. Sometimes the insults to your body and soul should be too great to bear alone, even in our safe and wealthy country. That's what has opened my eyes. As I walk in these late winter days, I watch all of you more closely now, for a little hitch in your strides, for a grimace quickly squelched. I know now that most likely a little animal is burrowing away inside, fate unknown. You are keeping it at bay.

And if that tall fellow over there, walking his poodle and looking so healthy, does get the big one, the terrible cancerous unconquerable complication hidden in brain or bone, let him scream like a blue jay in the spruce. He doesn't need to suck it up as if he were auditioning for the role of *Homo civilis*. For whom is he living at times like this, the species or the self?

Face Value

by Randy Osborne

"I don't expect you to remember me," she says. The Atlanta bar is loud around us. She's maybe late 30s, with dark hair and eyes, apple cheeks, a certain kind of defiance about the lips. She tells me her name, Jessica. "We were pen pals almost 20 years ago," she says.

I stare hard at her and ransack the mental files. Nothing. Later I will learn that Jessica heard my name from what turned out to be a mutual friend, who knew I'd be in the bar on this night for a special event. It's over and the crowd is shuffling out.

Jessica goes on, apparently untroubled by my blank stare. "You worked at *Creative Loafing*." Dimly I recall that job at the weekly alternative newspaper, but Jessica not at all. "I was a college student at Oglethorpe. I read one of your columns—something about family, I think—and sent you my poems. You wrote back."

She lowers her eyes. "I still have those letters. I just wanted you to know how much they meant to me." She was ready to quit writing in those days and I encouraged her, she says.

"Do you want to see them?"

*

In the past couple of years, I've started collecting old handwritten diaries and letters. The hobby arose as if out of nowhere, intense and mysterious. When asked to explain it, I tell people about my father.

Tom prowled yard sales for antiques he could mark up and resell. At his bank-teller job, he sorted bags of coins, plucking the rare finds and replacing them with his own pocket change, worth only face value. One of the first to own a metal detector, he haunted public parks on weekends, waving his wand like a dowsing rod. He unearthed tiny balls of tinfoil and flip-tops from soda cans, an occasional brooch pin or bauble.

One day as a toddler I stood at his side when he dumped onto the table his latest pile of flea-market junk. A hardcover book fell to the floor. When I opened it, the spine crackled. Spidery script in ancient ink lined the crumbly yellow pages. Wedged between them was a lock of hair, snipped and preserved more than a century before. I exhaled and the filaments trembled as if alive.

My spare bedroom is piled with crates full of folders and padded envelopes, the scribbled records of the pasts of strangers. Not that I plan to profit by passing them on. These I am keeping.

*

The scans arrive by email from Jessica. My letters, dated between June and November 1996, are not handwritten as I hoped but generated by an old-style dot-matrix printer, probably in *Creative Loafing*'s office. Most striking about them is how little my "correspondent" voice has changed, given all that history. Brisk, jaunty, self-deprecating. Is there an *essential me?* An immutable set of qualities that add up to an entity, myself, never to be mistaken for another?

As part of my day job—I'm a biotechnology journalist, handling the daily news of DNA and disease—I was assigned a few months ago to write about a saliva-based genetic test that purports to find predisposition to disease. I spat in the test tube.

"You have really good genes," the consultant told me after checking the results. Except for one hitch: one copy of the APOE3 gene, which confers an average risk for Alzheimer's disease, and one copy of the APOE4 gene, which means high risk. About 22 percent of the population bears this genotype, and it doubles my odds of Alzheimer's.

When I am held down screaming in some filthy public hospital (so I envision it) as the nurse finds a vein, what of that *essential me* will exist?

In one of the letters to Jessica, I mentioned that although she has referred to prose as a blind corridor, she did not go so far as to call it a brick wall. "Even those who pretend we know what we're doing are really groping along." I described my father's recent accident, which rendered him a paraplegic, and my fumbling attempts to handle his affairs. Maybe this is what prompted Jessica to send me an essay next, about her own father. "I like the way you folded into the second version of the truck-stop story how he is aging," went my reply. At the end, "Maybe I will get to meet you someday! That would be good. I have things to ask you about fiction vs. non-fiction, and the difficulties of each." How non-fiction can become fiction so easily, as recollections fail.

November 1996. In another year, the newspaper job would end. In two years, my wife would leave me a letter—also dot-matrix, in a business-sized envelope—on the pillow of the guest room where I had been sleeping. And then I was divorced.

*

They tow my decrepit Subaru from the parking deck of our apartment complex. Having misplaced the title, I avoided the hassle of getting new tags after I moved here from California. The truth is, I pretty much neglected the car altogether. Probably because of the flat tire, someone reported it as abandoned. I don't bother visiting the impound garage to harangue some bored clerk in his cage. What's a car anyway but the means of transport? Like the body hauls the soul around, until the soul alone is transported … somewhere. No doubt the Subaru will be auctioned or flattened for scrap, so I let my driver's license expire, too. My watch quits working and I throw it away. All of this I recognize as the wordless language of relinquishment.

I've waited a long time to get old. After high school, I knew that I needed more life in order to have anything worth saying to a blank page. I wanted to claw the calendar pages off in bunches and accumulate a past. I wanted to let time etch lines in my face and scorch my soul. It happened, but I don't know much more today than before, though I feel friendlier with the questions, more patient. Less patient, too, almost violently so, as the death clock ticks on. I'm pushing 60. It's not pushing back.

Still left to quit is my job. I phone a financial advisor to ask about retirement prospects. He wants a list of assets and I almost laugh. As he will, when he gets the "list." It's on the night after this conversation when shy Jessica sidles up to remind me about the letters.

"You did a good thing," she says.

I guess Jessica's age is about the same as mine when our letter exchange began. Such women look away from me in the street. Everyone understands this is instinct, simple biology, and nothing personal. Their DNA makes them not return my gaze for the same reason my DNA makes me hope (absurdly, because then what?) they will. Our respective strands of chromosomes, our stranded chromosomes, want only to replicate with the optimal candidate. For mine, they are it. For theirs, I am not.

Yet another, larger part of me feels a wash of relief at not much caring. The soul separates from the body, which is not much of a big deal. Can it be starting already? What's astounding, so lucky, is that they came together in the first place.

"A few years ago I ended a relationship that was murdering the joy out of me," Jessica writes in a follow-up email to the letter scans. Quickly she apologizes for the "melodrama."

She's "re-entering the world" and trying poetry again, she says. I tell her I'm glad. Her father has just turned 83, she adds. "My parents had kids late, which makes them the age of my friends' grandparents, which gives me an odd perspective sometimes." She mentions his "creeping Alzheimer's. At least he's still around, which I know isn't ever guaranteed, and everybody expected him to be gone by now."

*

One of my early letters to Jessica closed with, "I want to help and am running out of time." Another scrap of unintended melodrama, true in one way during the moment of composition—I was headed out the door, late for a flight—and more broadly true in another way now.

If I see her again, I'll tell her, since it's possible she will understand, about my stockpile of handwritten letters and diaries. About the form of treasure they make up for me in the language of those who've relinquished everything, happily or not. About how the once-blank pages are filled with insistent claims, clamoring to be heard, silently bursting with what we're expected to remember.

"Face Value" originally appeared in *Full Grown People.*

A Letter to Nick Ut

by Samantha Storey

Of all the images to come out of Saigon, your photo of the naked girl running toward the camera is the iconic one. It's easy to imagine you there in the humid dark corner of the day, one moment so quiet you can hear your breath panting in and out of your mouth, the camera bouncing off your flak jacket as you walked, and the next, a deafening blast, a wall of heat that shoves you back, and then the village, Trang Bang, wearing a swell of black oily smoke that climbed the sky.

First you saw the villagers running from the village, running toward you. A woman with her left leg badly burned by napalm, another carrying a baby with its skin coming off. But you didn't stop. You lifted your Leica to your eye, the sweat from your cheeks pressed against the black metal and your finger hopping up and down on the shutter. Then you saw the naked girl, and she was screaming, "Nong qua, nong qua" ("too hot, too hot"), as you photographed her running past, her back covered in burns. You were a Medusa of sorts, certainly not cruel and vengeful, but emboldened with super powers to stop time and turn her to stone.

You made her a monument. You made her *the* monument. She is everywhere now. She hangs in museums. She runs across the pages of history books. She is searched for and clicked on. Always she is in excruciating agony. And though you gave her the power to stop hearts, she still has not stopped wars. History repeats itself over and over. If she cannot stop it, who can? What can?

Contributors

Beth Bilderback is a writer living in Norfolk VA. She has work forthcoming in *KYSO Flash*.

Benjamin Cutler's poetry has appeared or is forthcoming in *Cold Mountain Review, Cumberland River Review, The Carolina Quarterly, Barren Magazine,* and *Longleaf Review,* among others. He won the North Carolina Poetry Society (NCPS) Carol Bessent Hayman Poetry of Love Contest, the NCPS Poetry of Witness Contest, and was a finalist for the NCPS Poet Laureate Award. Benjamin currently serves as the North Carolina Writers Network-West Swain County representative. His debut collection, *The Geese Who Might be Gods,* is available from Main Street Rag Publishing.

Lisa Dordal is the author of *Mosaic of the Dark* from Black Lawrence Press. She teaches in the English Department at Vanderbilt University. She is the recipient of an Academy of

American Poets University Prize and the Robert Watson Poetry Prize. Her poetry has appeared in *Best New Poets, Ninth Letter, CALYX, The Feminist Wire,* and *Nasty Women Poets: An Unapologetic Anthology of Subversive Verse.* Her website is lisadordal.com.

Steve Edwards lives in Massachusetts with his wife and young son. His writing can be found most recently in *Electric Literature No. 6, AGNI Online,* and *Silk Road Review.* He's currently at work on a new nonfiction book about his grandfather's appearance on the cover of LIFE Magazine in 1942. Educated at Purdue University and the University of Nebraska-Lincoln, Edwards works as an assistant professor of English Studies at Fitchburg State University.

Angie Ellis lives on Vancouver Island where she is finishing her first novel. Some of her work can be found in *Narrative Magazine, The Cincinnati Review, Grain Magazine,* and *The Forge Literary Magazine.* One of her stories was recently longlisted for the CBC Short Story Prize.

Valentina Gnup received her MFA in Creative Writing from Antioch University. She is the recipient of the *Rattle* Reader's Choice Award, the Barbara Mandigo Kelly Peace Poetry Award, the Joy Harjo Poetry Award, and the Mary Belle Campbell Book Award for her chapbook *Sparrow Octaves.* Her poems have appeared in many literary journals. She lives in Oakland, CA and teaches high school English. Her website is www.valentinagnup.com.

Jonathan Greenhause is a winner of *Aesthetica Magazine's* 2018 Creative Writing Award in Poetry and the 2017 Ledbury Poetry Competition. His poems have recently appeared or are forthcoming in *Columbia Poetry Review, Moon City Review, New Ohio Review, Redactions,* and *Salamander,* among others.

Alexandra Grimm holds an AB summa cum laude from Harvard College and an MFA from the University of New Hampshire. A native of the Finger Lakes, she is currently an MLIS student at Syracuse University. This is her first publication.

Kari Gunter-Seymour's poetry collections include *A Place So Deep Inside America It Can't Be Seen* (Sheila-Na-Gig Editions 2020) and *Serving* (Crisis Chronicles Press 2018/ 2020—Expanded Edition). Her poems appear in numerous journals and publications including *Verse Daily, Rattle, Still, The LA Times* and on her website: www.karigunterseymour-poet.com. She is the founder/executive director of the Women of Appalachia Project (WOAP) (www.womenofappalachia.com), and editor of the WOAP anthology series, *Women Speak,* volumes 1-6. She is the 2020 Ohio Poet of the Year and Poet Laureate of Ohio.

Pat Hale is the author of *Seeing Them with My Eyes Closed* and a chapbook, *Composition and Flight.* Her work appears in many journals and anthologies, and has been awarded

CALYX's Lois Cranston Memorial Poetry Prize, the Sunken Garden Poetry Prize, and first prize in the Al Savard Poetry Competition. She lives in West Hartford, serves on the board of directors for the Riverwood Poetry Series, and is currently a docent-in-training at the New Britain Museum of American Art.

Karen Paul Holmes has two poetry collections, *No Such Thing as Distance* and *Untying the Knot.* Her poems have been featured by Garrison Keillor on *The Writer's Almanac* and Tracy K. Smith on *The Slowdown.* Publications include *Prairie Schooner, Pedestal Magazine, Valparaiso Poetry Review, Diode Poetry Journal,* and many more. She founded and hosts the Side Door Poets in Atlanta, GA.

Jordana Jacobs is a middle and high school English teacher living in Brooklyn, NY. Her work has appeared in *Little Old Lady Comedy* and *Galaxy Brain.* This is her first published story.

Edison Jennings is a school bus driver for Head Start and the author of three chapbooks. Broadstone Books will publish his first full-length collection of poems, *Intentional Fallacies,* in 2021. He lives in Abingdon, Virginia.

Kyra Kondis is an MFA candidate in fiction at George Mason University and editor-in-chief of *So to Speak.* Some of her work can be found in *Wigleaf, Pithead Chapel, Jellyfish Review,* and on her website at kyrakondis.com.

Jim Krosschell divides his life into three parts: growing up for 29 years, working in science publishing for 29 years, and now writing in Massachusetts and Maine. His essays are widely published; a collection of those Maine-themed was published in *One Man's Maine* (May 2017) by Green Writers Press, which won a Maine Literary Award. His book *Owls Head Revisited* was published in 2015 by North Country Press.

Kathryn Kulpa is the author of a flash fiction chapbook, *Girls on Film*, and a short story collection, *Pleasant Drugs*. Her work can be found in *100 Word Story*, *Monkeybicycle*, *Smokelong Quarterly*, and other journals. Her stories were included in *Best Microfiction 2020*.

A.D. Lauren-Abunassar is an Arab-American writer who resides in New York. Her work has appeared or is forthcoming in *Poetry*, *Narrative*, *The Cincinnati Review*, *Diode*, *Radar Poetry*, and elsewhere. She was a 2020 Ruth Lilly & Dorothy Sargent Rosenberg finalist and the winner of the 2020 Palette Emerging Poet Contest. She is a graduate of the Iowa Writers' Workshop.

Katharyn Howd Machan, author of 38 poetry collections including *What the Piper Promised*, a national chapbook competition winner from Alexandria Quarterly Press, has taught Writing at Ithaca College since 1977. She coordinates the Ithaca Community Poets, directs the national Feminist

Women's Writing Workshops, Inc., and serves as Tompkins County's first poet laureate. Her poems have appeared in numerous magazines, anthologies, and textbooks, and she has edited three thematic anthologies, most recently, with Split Oak Press, a tribute collection celebrating the inspiration of Adrienne Rich.

Douglas W. Milliken is the author of two novels, *To Sleep as Animals* and *Our Shadows' Voice*, the collection *Blue of the World*, and several chapbooks, including *The Opposite of Prayer*. His stories have been honored by the Maine Literary Awards, the Pushcart Prize, and *Glimmer Train*, as well as published in dozens of journals, including *Slice*, *The Collagist*, and *The Believer*, among others.

Randy Osborne's essay collection, *Over the River and Stabbed to Death*, won the international Beverly Prize from Black Spring Publishing Group and is slated to appear in 2021. He lives in Atlanta.

Simon Perchik is an attorney whose poems have appeared in *Partisan Review*, *Forge*, *Poetry*, *Osiris*, *The New Yorker*, and elsewhere. His most recent collection is *The Osiris Poems*, published by boxofchalk in 2017.

Jeff Somers has published nine novels, including the Avery Cates Series of noir-science fiction novels and the Ustari Cycle series of urban fantasy novels. His short story "Ringing the Changes" was selected for inclusion in *Best American*

Mystery Stories 2006. He also writes about books for Barnes and Noble and about the craft of writing for *Writer's Digest*, which published his book on the craft of writing *Writing Without Rules* in 2018.

Samantha Storey is a writer and journalist. Her work has appeared in *The New York Times, HuffPost, Seattle Weekly, Colorado Review* and *The Lascaux Review*. She was a 2015 recipient of an emerging writer fellowship from the Center for Fiction. She lives in Brooklyn, NY with her family, and she is currently at work on a novel.

Made in the USA
Middletown, DE
29 January 2021